Cold. Cold. Cold. Cold. Cold. Cold. Cold. Cold. Cold.

Published by Lucky Duck Books | www.luckyduckbook.com
ISBN 9798895896518
The illustrations were created digitally.
Book design by Lindsay Ward.

STOP
THE
SNOW
Frank Tupta + Lindsay Ward

It's a snow day!
Hip, hip, hooray!

Grab your hat, grab your gloves, grab your sled! Grab your...

…Baby Sloth?
You again?!

Cold. Cold. Cold.

That's not enough snow.
Hey, Kid! Can you SHAKE the book to make more snow?

I'm stuck!
Hmmm...try SHAKING the book a little more.

SHAKE the book even HARDER!

Too much!
Uh-oh...
KEEP SHAKING!

Ahhhhhhh

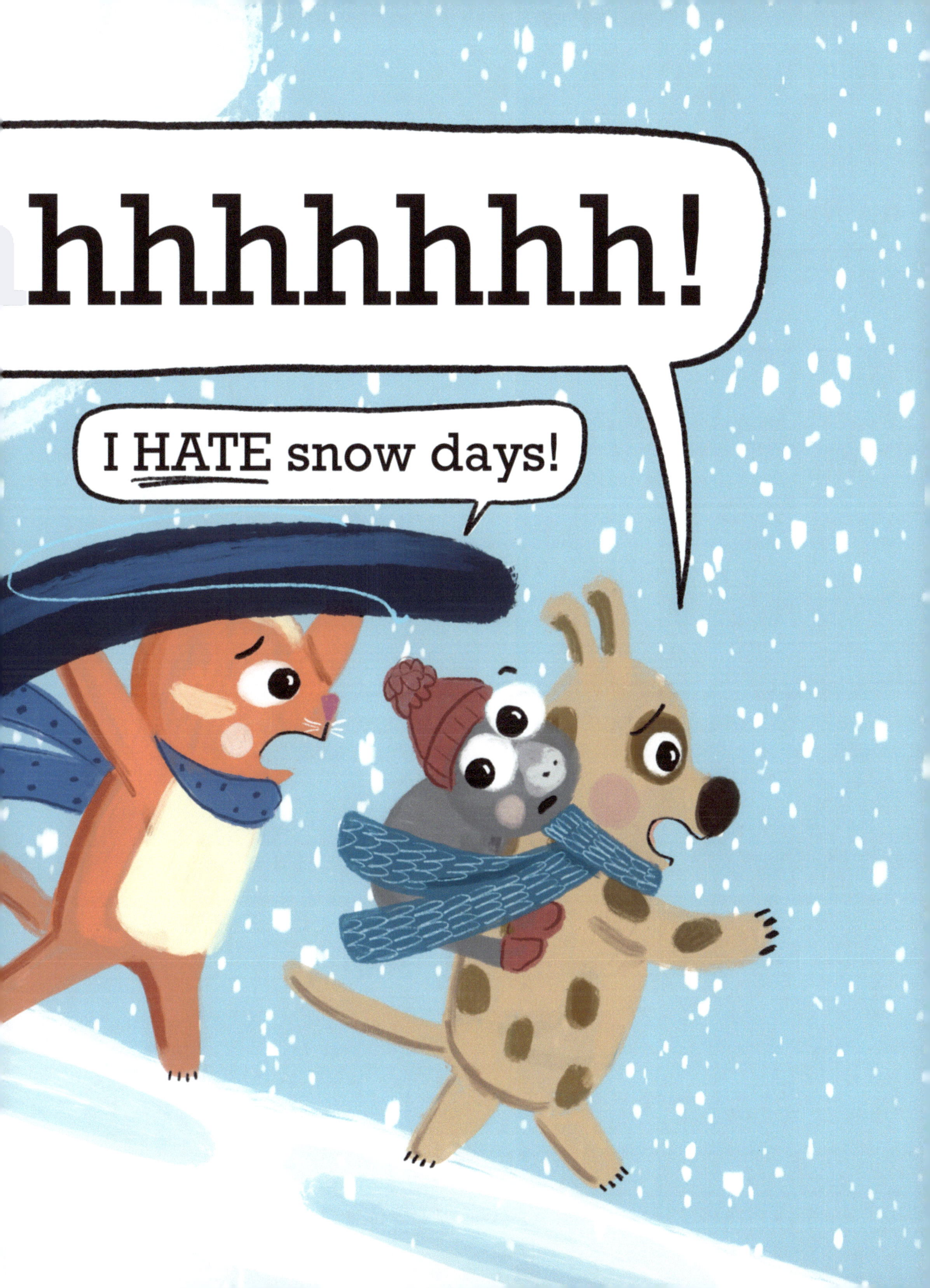

hhhhhhh!
I HATE snow days!

I can't see anything!
Cold. Cold. Cold. Cold.

Me neither!

Yikes! Try BLOWING off the snow.

BLOW a little harder.

Wow! That was super, duper, pooper hard. Great job!
Pooper?

What's that sound?
Oh…snow….

It's a snowmageddon! Quick! TURN the page!

You turned too fast!

IT'S EVERYWHERE!
What are we going to do?

STOP
THE SNOW!

Quick! SHAKE the book as hard as you can and then SPIN the book around in a circle!

No more spin cycle.

I don't feel
so good...

TILT the book → **and TURN the page.**

You wanted snow,
you got it....

Are you thinking what I'm thinking?

Woo

-hoo!

Oh no! Oh no! Oh no! Oh no!

Best...
...snow day...
...EVER!

www.ingramcontent.com/pod-product-compliance
Lightning Source LLC
Chambersburg PA
CBHW041645110726
48005CB00003B/715